1906 San Francisco Earthquake

A Captivating Guide to the Deadliest Earthquake in the History of the United States

Free Bonus from Captivating History
(Available for a Limited time)

Hi History Lovers!

Now you have a chance to join our exclusive history list so you can get your first history ebook for free as well as discounts and a potential to get more history books for free! Simply visit the link below to join.

Captivatinghistory.com/ebook

Also, make sure to follow us on Facebook, Twitter and Youtube by searching for Captivating History.

Contents

Introduction

When we think of the solid earth under our feet, it gives us a sense of security and stability. But what happens when that seeming stability suddenly heaves up and literally shakes the foundations of a whole city and every living thing in it?

Earthquakes are not a new phenomenon, and many people have survived seismic events of varying intensity. But those who felt the intensity of the 1906 earthquake in San Francisco and its tragic aftermath experienced a catastrophe to which few, if any in history, could relate.

By the early 1900s, San Francisco had gone through decades of transformation, turning itself into a bustling city known as the "gateway to the Pacific." Between its busy coastal ports, thriving entertainment scene, and a strengthening military presence, San Francisco had gained a reputation as an important hub in the western United States. But as we are all too aware, disasters, especially those of the natural variety, strike indiscriminately, caring little for what humans consider valuable—including their lives and those of their families.

Though the city itself was damaged—buildings fell and burned, streets heaved and cracked—it's those within the city whose stories we find the most compelling. That earthquake in 1906 shook a city to its foundations, but it also shook the lives of real people, some of whom did not survive the initial quake or the fires that followed.

We'll walk through not only the facts and timeline of this historic earthquake but allow those that were there to continue to "tell" their stories. Eyewitness accounts have painted a picture of seemingly unstoppable catastrophes piled on top of one another, split-second decisions that saved lives, other decisions that led to further disaster, and the helplessness of many to control the fate of themselves or the city. We'll recount stories of heroism alongside heartbreak, the dangers that followed the initial quake and aftershocks, the relief response from those who came to help, and how San Francisco started to rebuild itself from the ashes of a disaster.

As you read the accounts of what happened, imagine yourself in the picture as the quake happened. Would you have been on a ship at sea, on the commuter train, working on your farm, or violently shaken from your bed the moment the quake occurred? Would you have thought quickly on your feet to escape, run to save others, or prayed out of fear? They are questions that are hard to answer.

Chapter 1 – The Earth Shifts

On April 18th, 1906, the early morning streets of San Francisco were quiet, as they were on most days. The noise and fanfare of the previous night's opera and vaudeville shows had died down, with theatergoers long gone home, waiting to soon wake to the new day. Though everything was still on the surface, out to sea, about ten miles deep within the earth, the San Andreas Fault was about to slip.

One hundred and fifty miles from San Francisco, the crew of the schooner *John A. Campbell* were asleep in their bunks as their ship cut its way through the Pacific Ocean. Without a moment's notice, below the ocean bed, an incredible energy was unleashed—a force that exceeded all the explosive power used during World War II. As the schooner rose and crashed back down into the sea, the alarmed crew were jolted from their beds. Understandably thinking the boat had rammed into a shipwreck or perhaps a whale, they hastened to the deck. But when the puzzled captain and crew looked over the rails, there was nothing to be seen.

The shockwave, moving through the sea at two miles per second, did not take long to reach the steamer ship *Argo*, which was easily cruising through the calm sea. The shockwave shot through the water forty fathoms below, causing the ship to shudder suddenly and severely. Like the crew of the *John A. Campbell*, those aboard the

Argo were caught completely off guard and assumed that their ship had struck something like a reef or a raft of floating logs. The jolt buckled the sturdy ship's steel plates, and bolts were forcefully blown out of their riveting. For one horrifying moment, her captain believed that his whole ship was breaking apart. Like the schooner's baffled crew, when the *Argo*'s men checked the sea, there was nothing in sight but ocean. By the time they looked out into the open expanse, the earthquake was already reaching land.

Near the shore, the tide gauge registered a rather small tsunami wave measuring about three inches in height. An extraordinarily unimpressive blip, it gave no indication of the force that was about to be unleashed onto the shore.

At seven thousand miles per hour, the power unleashed by the earthquake blasted into the California shoreline, frighteningly close to the Point Arena lighthouse.[1] The force caused the structure, which stood 110 feet tall, to sway frantically on its base. Though it had withstood decades of ferocious weather, the lantern of the lighthouse beacon easily cracked and shattered, raining a shimmer of glass down to its floor.

As the incredible force continued south, animals in the region sensed the coming shift right before it hit, becoming restless and agitated. Horses kicked about in their corrals. A milk cart rattled loudly as the milkman tried to calm his excited horse.

The human population near San Francisco, though, had no inkling of what was coming. Brigadier General Frederick Funston, the commander of the Presidio military outpost at the time, said that before the quake, there was "not a single sound" of warning— "no shrieking of whistles, no clanging of bells."

But it was within the city where some of the most dramatic scenes unfolded and damages were felt.

---

[1] The Point Arena lighthouse is ninety miles north of San Francisco.

4

Chapter 2 – A City Shakes

At 5:12 a.m., a significant foreshock jolted the ground underneath the city of San Francisco. If this was not enough to grab the attention of those within the city, what was about to come shook everyone and everything to their very foundations. About twenty to twenty-five seconds after the initial shock, the full force of the quake rolled through the ground and was felt in all its 8.0 magnitude of intensity.[2] The energy released underneath was terrifying in its power.

Both those sleeping and awake were thrown into an immediate panic, and anyone who was able to gain their footing stumbled about, terrified. Their floors heaved, and the walls around them shook, and the people instinctively sought safety, with many running into the street in various states of dress, leaving their valuables behind.

In recounting how it sounded and felt, John Farish, a mining engineer staying at the St. Francis Hotel, said that he woke up to a loud rumbling. He compared it to "a strong wind rushing through a forest mixed with waves breaking against a cliff." Farish referred to the main quake as a "concussion" type explosion, like that of "a huge blast" that "shook the building to its foundations."

---

[2] Though the earthquake is generally said to have been an 8.0 on the seismological Richter scale, various sources value it from as low as 7.7 to as high as 8.3 on the Richter scale.

As frightened people poured into the street, screams of terror rose up around the city. Others fell into feverish prayer, fearing that a divine judgment had fallen upon the city. With the church bells shaking and clanging in a violent cacophony, no one could blame a soul for thinking that the end had come. The furious ringing created an ominous soundtrack, a chaotic backdrop as chimneys toppled onto their houses and through roofs, crushing some as they still lay in their beds. Towers crashed down from their heights, and entire walls crumbled into the streets. This violent shock lasted for about a minute—a minute that must have felt unending to those experiencing it.

Simple wood-frame houses were no match for the violent quaking, their timbers splintering and the structures they held collapsing into rubble. Large gas reservoirs and sprawling factory buildings did not fare much better. This was exemplified over at the city's gas and electric company buildings, where a tall smokestack at one of the stations toppled, killing a man in the company's yard. Warehouse walls cracked and bulged, threatening to snap. Buildings that stayed upright shifted from their foundation by two or three feet.

The streets themselves heaved up and split apart as if with gaping wounds. Future police commissioner Jesse Cook heard what he described as a "deep and terrible" rumble. As he turned to look down the street, he watched in horror as the street rose up and undulated, rolling toward him like ocean waves.

Produce dealers, with their wagons on the streets, were thrown about as the ground heaved. Some carts toppled over, still hitched to their horses, with drivers and animals lying dead in the streets.

Underground, gas and water mains ruptured, releasing deadly gas and floods of water into the streets. Telegraph poles rocked back and forth, creating a tangle of sparking wires that lay twisted together along with electrical lines.

The unusual rotary motion of the quake caused seemingly unbendable structures like steel streetcar rails, underground pipelines, bridges, and others to become unimaginably twisted and mangled. Metal squealed and ground out of its original shapes. The twelve-story Call building, a steel skyscraper, shifted off its base by two feet, its insides twisted by the force.

Over at the Bush Street fire station, San Francisco Fire Chief Dennis Sullivan was asleep in his third-floor residence. When the quake struck, he leaped to his feet and ran toward his wife in the adjoining room. At the same moment, the smokestacks high atop the neighboring California Hotel collapsed, sending a mass of brick and mortar crashing through the station roof. The wave of heavy debris carried Chief Sullivan and his wife with it right through to the first floor, mortally wounding the chief. Unfortunately, Sullivan did not recover from the severe chest and head injuries sustained in the collapse and tragically died three days later. It was a loss that was to be more deeply felt in the coming days.

Chaotic scenes like this quickly unfolded across the entire city and just outside of it, which was where the San Francisco commuter train was making its way to the city. The two jolts caused the engine car to jackknife along with four other cars. The rest of the train swayed back and forth wildly, forcing wheels to come off and toppling its cars onto their sides. Dairy farmers milking their cattle were thrown to the ground as the frightened animals stampeded, with the cows becoming so traumatized that they couldn't give milk for days.

Though the biggest shock went on for about a minute, relatively smaller shocks, some as big as 6.4 on the Richter scale, continued to rock the city until noon. The severity of the initial quakes and the smaller shocks that followed was enough to destroy the center of the city. It is unclear how many died that morning, but the earthquake proved to be just the beginning, and unbelievably, it was the less destructive part of the disaster.

Chapter 3 – Infernos Consume

It wasn't long before columns of smoke began to appear around the city. In the business district, four separate fires reared up around the mostly brick buildings, some of which were considered to be "fireproof."

General Frederick Funston wasted no time springing into action, rushing toward the fires burning on Sansome and California Streets. It was not even 6 a.m., and the crisis looming from the fire was already evident. The city's firemen, who were without a chief, were still on the scene by the time the general arrived, but they had another crisis to contend with—a lack of water. Water main breaks caused by the earthquake compounded the problem of an already inadequate water system.

General Funston immediately saw that the firemen, as well as the police, would need the help of troops at nearby outposts. With no other way of getting a message to his men, he "wildly dashed about" as he tried to flag down passing motorists, all of whom ignored his desperate gesticulating. He was forced to run to the nearest army stables and send messages around the city for all available men to report to Police Chief Jeremiah Dinan at the Hall of Justice.

By the time 9 a.m. came around, citizens, as well as authorities, began to see the stark reality that the city was burning. Hundreds of fires were rapidly springing up around the city, even claiming some of the strongest buildings that had initially withstood the earthquake. The fires surrounded and attacked everything, including the tallest skyscrapers in the city.

Flames shot out wildly from the windows of large hotels and smaller lodging houses alike, triumphantly claiming them all and leaving only charred walls as a reminder of what once stood there. As flames marched toward the Palace Hotel, a longtime favorite of those visiting the city, guests quickly fled and with little time to spare. Curls of fire soon reached the building and turned it into an inferno before moving on to its neighboring structures.

Unsurprisingly, the area of the city that housed its newspaper offices also quickly came under threat. Though the Examiner Building had collapsed in the earthquake, the sturdier Chronicle Building remained standing. But full of papery ammunition, the buildings became tinderboxes, unable to withstand the fiery assault.

Many watched helplessly as landmark after landmark was claimed by the flames. The Grand Opera, the Emporium, St. Ignatius Church, the Bohemian Club, and many others represented tremendous losses to San Francisco's financial, art, and religious communities.

Even more distressing than seeing important city buildings disappear was watching their own residences burn. The fire claimed mansions and humble wooden structures alike.

Since the fires had moved swiftly from house to house and neighborhood to neighborhood, many had no time to save any of their belongings and were in the street with little more than the clothes on their backs. Some who were able to grab their valuables threw them in ditches or covered holes to try to protect them from the flames, setting up crude markers in order to find and retrieve their things after the fire had passed. Others tried to move their things to safer locations, dragging overloaded trunks through the streets with ropes and carrying blankets, boxes, and even pets in their arms as they tried to rush away, unsure as to where they would go. Those who could find a wagon to hire to take their belongings would have paid exorbitant prices for the luxury.

Not all buildings were lost, however. The heroic persistence of firefighters and citizens saved many structures. Maybe the most remarkable example of this was the United States Mint, which housed millions of dollars in gold and silver.

Frank Leach, the superintendent, along with several other male employees, raced to the Mint following the initial quake. Men were stationed on every floor of the building, including the basement and roof. Using the Mint's fire apparatus and hoses, employees and firemen took turns laboriously hand pumping water from the basement.

The victory over the fire was far from sure, though. The fires were reducing the surrounding buildings to charcoal and looked to claim the Mint next. Flames licked at the windows and pushed their way through the rear of the building, forcing the people to temporarily retreat. The workers found their ground and fought back. For seven grueling hours, they fought, hosing down windows and the roof and swiftly putting out smaller fires that sprang up, keeping them from growing into monstrous infernos. In the end, the quick thinking of the employees and the tireless efforts of all on the scene managed to score a victory for the building. Though it did not remain unscathed, the damage was minor, especially compared to the surrounding neighborhood.

Elsewhere, police officers and detectives employed bravery and resourcefulness to save what they could from the Hall of Justice. There came a point in the morning where it was obvious to the men that the Hall could not be saved from the fire. But that didn't mean they wouldn't try to save all the important police records contained within. A detail of officers was assigned to quickly move the files to Portsmouth Square. They covered the records with a canvas, hoping to protect it from ash and other elements, and kept vigil over the collection. Supplied with ample courage and other provisions, they still lacked access to the one thing that they needed the most—water.

The fire rapidly moved toward the square, surrounding it and keeping the officers trapped in the area. Fiery cinders rained down on the canvas covering the records, and the men fought through the intense heat to beat down the fires that ignited. It was only a temporary band-aid, though. Without water, the records would be lost. Desperate to find something they could use to quench the flames, officers ran into a nearby bar, grabbing all the bottles of beer they could find. For twenty-four hours, they doused the canvas with beer, dampening the embers that fell, and in the end, they managed to save the valuable records for which they had fought so hard.

The officers at Plymouth Square were not the only ones to use everything at their disposal to save what was important to them. Directly following the quake, some in the city had the forethought to fill up their bathtub with buckets of water, likely relieved that they were later able to use those reserves to squelch the fires that threatened their homes. Others without water reserves used wine and vinegar to save their residences, dousing flames that tried to take their humble houses.

At some point, every fire company in the city faced the same devastating problem—broken water mains and lack of water sources typically used to fight fires. Like others in similar situations around the city, it didn't stop them from using ingenuity and resourcefulness to continue the fight.

When the water mains broke, all that water went somewhere, with tens of thousands of gallons ponding in the sewers. Firemen dropped hoses into every pool of water they could reach, eventually draining their sources. Firemen also tapped into the city's 23 water cisterns, which gave them up to possibly 100,000 gallons to use in the fight.

Another saving grace for the city was the fact that a portion of it sat on or near the waterfront. Firemen dropped hoses into the bay and were able to save many buildings in the area due to its endless water supply. Yet, this, too, had its limits. Eventually, fires burned outside the reach of the bay water hoses, and firemen were forced to find other solutions.

The bravery and tenacity of those who fought the fires are well documented, and many fought until they collapsed and could give no more. Water, wine, vinegar, beer, and other liquids all played a part in saving the city from complete devastation, but the firemen realized that it still wouldn't be enough. They needed to use one more resource at their disposal—dynamite.

Chapter 4 – The Dynamite Solution

Fear began to mount that the conflagrations around the city might not be able to be controlled. Disaster loomed. Fighting the fires would test the best of the city's firemen with a job that seemed all but hopeless. City authorities finally concluded that the only hope for taming the fires would come from using dynamite.

Much like controlled fire breaks created by wildfire fighters today, San Francisco authorities believed that they could halt the progress of the fires by taking away the source of fuel. Troops and firemen would get ahead of the flames and blow up buildings in the fire's path, leaving little for the fire to consume and interrupting the path of travel.

General Frederick Funston wasted no time organizing this endeavor. He mobilized troops, firefighters, and police officers alike, sending them out around the city to strategically create the fire breaks. Their plan was quickly put into effect, and it wasn't long before thunderous explosions were being heard around the city.

The men did not go into this planning to demolish every building near a fire. They proceeded carefully at first, blowing up one or two buildings at a time, hoping to keep the damage to a minimum. Such caution proved to be ineffective against the determined and swiftly moving infernos. The men upped their measures and took down half of a block at a time, but this, too, was proving to be too little. Flames continued to leap over rubble and through the newly made gaps between buildings. Dynamite squads had no choice but to take dynamite to whole city blocks, taking a scorched-earth approach and leveling everything. Everything the explosives touched was blown to dust.

As dangerous as it was to fight the fires that raged around the city, being part of an explosives team was exponentially more so. This is illustrated by the story of Lieutenant Charles Pulis, the commander of one of the city's Light Artillery companies.

In charge of dynamiting the Sixth and Jesse street blocks, he and Police Captain Henry Gleeson laid the heavy charges inside of a building. According to police records from the time, Pulis lit the fuse, and both men fled toward the door. They wouldn't make it out on time. Unable to beat the swiftly burning fuse, the explosion blew the men out of the building and into the street. Wreckage from the blast rained down on their unconscious forms. Pulis's injuries were severe. Besides a fractured skull, he broke several other bones and sustained internal injuries. Though it was a near-fatal incident, both men survived.

Amid incidents like that of Lieutenant Pulis and Captain Gleeson, it was obvious that dynamite in the hands of the untrained was not only extremely dangerous but also did not prove to be as effective as they hoped. In some cases, it caused more harm than good. Yet, with the life of the city on the line, this was too important to be left to volunteers ignorant in the proper use of these explosives. It was time to bring in the experts.

Three skilled explosives engineers, the best and most trusted, were selected from the Mare Island Naval Shipyard by Admiral Bowman McCalla. With Captain McBride in charge of two gunners, the trio made up the city's new ace dynamite squad.

The men were ordered to stop the flames without regard to the cost of property damage. With the flames continuing to spread, there was no other choice—it was the only way to salvage the doomed city. But if they were going to stop an out-of-control conflagration, they would need the firepower to match it.

With the agreement of city authorities, the trio decided to make their stand on Van Ness Avenue. Fires from the burning business district quickly made their way toward them. Though none of the buildings in that area had yet been touched by flames or embers, they couldn't be allowed to remain standing. There was no time to waste if the trio wanted to cut it off. Systematically, they set their charges. Terrifying, powerful thunder reverberated through the area as the explosives took down one block after another. Not a building remained standing.

When the dynamite and guncotton were done with their work, a million dollars in debris and dust formed a gaping firebreak. The fire made its approach and reached its tentacles out to the ruins. It can only be imaged how everyone present held their collective breaths as the flames reached the debris field. Though there was some fuel for the fire among the wreckage, it was not enough to feed the hungry flames for long. Water pumped from the bay helped complete the mission. The fires that once raged wild soon burned what little they could and then died amid what remained of the neighborhood.

Though the dynamite did its share in stopping the fires near Van Ness Avenue, the real credit went to the dynamite squad trio. Their skillful and courageous efforts were what halted the main conflagration, and their heroic efforts are credited with saving the city from total fiery destruction. Though they made history, once their work was done, the three men quietly departed, leaving the weary firemen to watch over the smoldering ruins.

Chapter 5 – Eyewitnesses Tell Their Stories

While firemen, police officers, and soldiers quickly mobilized around the city and gave reports of what they did and saw, many ordinary citizens had harrowing tales of their own. Some, like those in the following accounts, were struck with terror as they were shaken from their beds. What they described were near apocalyptic scenes. Here are some of their stories.

Businessman **Jerome Clark** started his story from a vantage point outside the city proper. As he lived across the San Francisco Bay, he only felt minor quakes at home early that morning. Unaware of what was happening on the other side of the bay, he took his usual commuter ferry to the city. As he stepped off the ferry, he was met with a cataclysmic scene. He described flames seething in every direction that he looked.

As he stood gazing, slowly taking in the scene, a nearby five-story building succumbed to the flames and came crashing down. The downward force of the crash acted as a fan, sweeping flames across Market Street, where they laid claim to one of the new "fireproof" buildings. As he turned his attention to the street itself, he saw that the earthquake had caused it to sink three or four feet in some areas while rising in cracked, mishappen humps four or five feet high in other areas.

G. A. Raymond was a guest at the Palace Hotel, and he was still asleep when the earthquake struck. As he woke up, he was thrown out of his bed by the massive jolt. Trying to find his footing, he fell as the floor shook violently. Leaving the $600 in gold he had stashed under his pillow, he grabbed his clothing and ran to the lobby. Suddenly, the lights went out, and he rushed to the door along with others.

Once outside, he witnessed "a sight that he never wanted to see again." He looked up into the dawning light to see an ominous sight— a sky raining stones. They fell all around him, crushing many to death. Huge buildings swayed like grass in the breeze, and a sound that he described as "100 cannons going off at one time" filled the air. Fire shot out from various buildings.

Unsure what was happening, he asked the man next to him. Before the man could even get the words out, "a thousand bricks fell" on the man, killing him before Raymond's eyes. Raymond fled in a panic, with people all around him crying, calling for help, and even praying, thinking it was the actual end of the world.

As he ran, he met a Catholic priest who urged Raymond to follow him to the ferry. They rushed down the street, witnessing young and old being crushed under falling debris while others crawled out from under already fallen debris.

Streets cracked and opened into gaping chasms. A frightened drove of cattle rushed past Raymond and disappeared. Moving closer to where he last saw them, he peered over the edge of one of the chasms. He could see that they had indeed fallen and been swallowed into the abyss-like fissures. These sights made him "crazy with fear."

John Barrett, who, at the time, was the news editor for the *San Francisco Examiner*, tells a similar story of the scene that unfolded during the quake. He described the initial seconds of the quake as feeling like the "earth slipping gently from under his feet," causing him to stagger and reel. As the quake intensified, the "sickening swaying" caused him to fall in the street, unable to regain his footing. He later described it as feeling unable to move, as if suctioned to the earth by a huge vacuum. All around him, people were on all fours "like crawling bugs."

As buildings crumbled around him, Barrett felt as though his "head was split with the roar that crashed" in his ears. He saw an ironworker on his way to the Union Iron Works. A cornice from the building he stood near toppled down, crushing the unfortunate man with his dinner pail still in hand.

Though it seemed near an eternity, the main quake soon ended. As Barrett tried to return to his feet, the aftershocks that immediately followed continued to send him reeling. Once the shaking stopped, he could see the damage through the dust clouds darkening the sky.

Everything around him lay twisted and mangled, the streets gaping wide open. He could smell gas from the broken main. Then rose "a horrible chorus of human cries of agony" as families lay buried in the rubble of their homes and fires began to burn around the city.

Barrett returned to his feet, looked at his colleagues, and proclaimed, "This is going to be a hell of a day." Little did he know how prophetic those words would turn out to be. Describing the hellish scene playing out around the city, he later recalled it as one of "agony, death, and a flaming torch," as if "some fire demon" rushed around, setting everything ablaze. The fire shot up everywhere, yet the flaming destruction was just beginning.

Chapter 6 – Tales of Heroism and Heartbreak

Though heroic by their very nature, firemen, soldiers, sailors, and police officers were not the only ones to show courage and strength during this emergency. Ordinary citizens, at times working alongside professionals, showed incredible bravery and compassion toward others.

Many were rescued from crumbled buildings and unstoppable fires, but there were also many heartbreaking instances of those who could not be saved in time. The following accounts illustrate the many scenes that occurred across the city.

On Folsom Street, one man was fortunate enough to be saved from the wreckage of a lodging house. Two other men inside did not fare as well. Before he got out, he heard their conversation:

"I'm not hurt, but there's a beam across my back, and I can't get out from under it."

The second man responded, "I'm caught too; it's my wrist. Don't worry; they'll get us out."

The heartrending optimism of the men is hard to read about since before rescuers could dig them from where they were trapped, the fires came and forced the rescuers to retreat. Helplessly, rescuers watched as the fire leaped into the wreckage, claiming everything and everyone inside.

Some heroic deeds required exceptional strength and courage to carry out as they came at a high cost. Eyewitness Max Fast watched as the Windsor Hotel caught fire. Three men went to the roof to get away from the inferno inside, but once there, they were trapped with no way down. Seeing their panic and understanding the terrible fiery fate that awaited them, a military officer on the scene had a hard decision to make. Wanting to save them from further agony, he felt giving them a painless death was the kinder option. And so, he ordered his men to shoot them as five thousand people looked on.

Those officers were not the only ones that had to make a painful decision like this. Eyewitness Adolphus Busch also described a chilling scene, which he said was the most terrible thing he ever saw. Policemen and citizens worked urgently to rescue a man who was pinned by the wreckage of a building. The trapped man watched in silent terror as the flames crept closer, eventually reaching his feet. As the fire began to burn him, the man begged the police officer to kill him, saving him from an even worse fate. After taking down the man's name and address, the officer pulled out his gun and, squeezing the trigger, shot the man in the head, killing him and instantly ending his suffering.

At the bottom of the Russian Hill area, an affluent neighborhood, stood small frame houses occupied by immigrants. Without bias or reservation, an army corps volunteer moved quickly to try to outrun the fire and warned people of the flames swiftly coming toward them and their humble homes. The flames were too fast, however. Before they could get out of an old frame house, three women became trapped on the top floor. The building was a virtual tinderbox waiting to ignite. Thinking quickly on his feet, a man tore up a piece of fencing and used it to climb to the window where the distressed women huddled. He managed to grab two of the women and slid them down the rail. They reached the ground, injured but safe. The fire reached the roof and spread quickly. The man struggled to quickly save the last woman, but as he did, both fell into the flames and were consumed.

Accounts like these occurred all over the city. Sailors formed firefighting task forces and leaped into action. Firemen battled for thirty-six hours, strained under the weight of conditions they had never even imagined facing, let alone having experienced before.

It's not possible to contain all the stories of heroism and heartrending loss in one place. Firemen, in particular, worked tirelessly and selflessly to save the city and their fellow citizens, knowing their own homes had been destroyed and going without sleep, with little food or water, and without even knowing what happened to their own families.

However, it wasn't just fire that threatened the city. There was also a difficult and thankless task that fell to the patrolling sentries—protecting the city from crime.

Chapter 7 – Crime Curbed Through Violence

"As it has come to my attention that thieves are taking advantage of the present deplorable conditions and are plying their nefarious vocations among the ruins in our city, all peace officers are ordered to instantly kill anyone caught looting or committing any other serious crimes."

—E. E. Schmitz, Mayor

Not all in the city showed a heroic nature during this time of crisis. Criminals took advantage of the chaos to loot and commit other crimes. Authorities were certainly aware that unsavory opportunists would engage in criminal activities, and so, they swiftly moved into action. Within mere hours of the quake, San Francisco Mayor Eugene Schmitz drafted and posted a proclamation that could give additional temptation to looters. He directed that gas and electricity be turned off indefinitely, plunging the city into total darkness at night.

Though the proclamation also instituted a citywide curfew that commanded people to stay home from dark until daylight, the mayor knew the order would not be obeyed by all. Knowing that looters would find the darkness of night to be far too tempting, the mayor gave them a reason to take pause. In a declaration that many found shocking, the proclamation ordered federal troops, city police officers, and special officers to "kill any and all persons" found not just looting but also committing any other crime.

This warning was no mere idle threat. In a stark demonstration of what happened to those who dared defy the law, the body of a man shot by authorities was thrown atop a pile of bricks and stones, the bullet hole in his chest visible to all. Pinned to his chest was a chilling sign that sternly cautioned, "Take warning!"

Others also reported seeing dead bodies left lying in the streets where they fell, each with a placard that read "shot for stealing" or "Looter." It was obvious that crime would not be tolerated and that justice would be swiftly and summarily executed on the spot.

The stiff penalty for crime aside, citizens now believed that the proclamation was also a declaration to suspend constitutional law and institute martial law throughout the city. Most did not realize that the mayor had neither actually declared martial law nor had the power to do so, and those that did have the power (the governor and President Theodore Roosevelt) had not declared it. However, the city was too busy fighting the rising crisis to protest a move that many would later declare unconstitutional or even dictatorial.

Though it may have created some confusion among authorities as to who actually had control of the city, most citizens felt reassured by the heavy police and military presence. However, not everyone took comfort from that. Journalist Henry Anderson Lafler lamented the atmosphere that descended upon the city that had been brought on by the presence of so many soldiers. He likened the atmosphere to a medieval siege—a "city captured in war." Later, he bemoaned the situation, saying that the people had "been suddenly gripped by the throat by a stupid soldiery and held fast" while the city burned. For others, the morning bugle calls, the pacing sentry patrols, and the officers on horseback only added to the perception that the city was under military occupation.

Yet, the widespread perception that the authorities had the city under control could not be underestimated in its effectiveness. The sight of soldiers with bayoneted guns marching through the streets was an unspoken signal to citizens that order would be kept.

Despite the explicit warnings and the presence of one thousand patrolmen from various branches of the police and military, some unscrupulous individuals remained undeterred.[3] One of the most unsettling and unspeakable crimes occurring around the city was the robbing of the dead—a crime seemingly easy to get away with in the middle of a burning city. Witnesses recounted stories of those who found out how strictly the law was enforced and how "justice" was meted out without mercy. Soldiers did not hesitate to "shoot down the ghouls" who dared desecrate the dead.

This is illustrated in the story of one citizen who witnessed a man trying to cut the stiffened fingers off a dead woman in an attempt to steal her rings. Three soldiers saw what he was doing and, chasing the man, ordered him to put his hands in the air. Instead, the would-be robber drew his gun. The soldiers, backed up by six policemen, immediately raised their rifles and fired, hitting the man with nine bullets. His body was then unceremoniously taken to an alley and disposed of on the cement.

In a separate incident, a thief found a young woman who had fainted, lying unconscious on the floor of a hotel. Instead of trying to simply take the rings off her fingers, the brute cut off her finger and ran, leaving her helpless to the ravages of the nearing fire. Though he escaped any well-deserved justice, it demonstrated the "ghoulish" nature that some allowed themselves to fall into.

---

[3] Though criminal acts still took place, the heavy patrol presence did have a positive effect. Many citizens were documented noting that crime, especially the robbing of the dead, would have been "many more times prevalent were it not for the constant vigilance on all sides, as well as the summary justice."

These would not be isolated happenings. A group of fourteen men found the empty US Mint building too enticing of an opportunity to pass up. They hatched a plot and brazenly attempted to break into and steal the unattended money, counting on authorities being distracted elsewhere. They underestimated the vigilance of those on duty, though. During the attempt, they were shot down by a guard after refusing to comply with his command to cease and desist.

Eyewitnesses recounted many stories of thieves being shot or, even more gruesomely, run through with bayonets while in the act of stealing. For instance, a sailor patrolling Market Street saw a man digging through the ruins of a jewelry shop, apparently intent on stealing what he found. Upon seeing him, the sailor shot at the man three times, but the man somehow remained untouched and ran. The sailor chased after him and ran the man through with his bayonet, bringing him to the ground.

Not all such enforcements of the mayor's proclamation happened in the moment. Three thieves who were caught in three separate crimes were taken before a crowd of ten thousand people, where they were lined up and shot. It made the seriousness of the order hard to deny.

Some soldiers had an excessively strict interpretation of the law against stealing and looting. They also extended this to those who tried to take advantage of the situation by price gouging. This was evidenced in the case of a beer delivery man who agreed to transport a family and their belongings. When they got to their destination, the driver demanded that he be paid twenty-five dollars, which was much higher than the normal rate. The man who hitched a ride was down to his last five dollars and offered it to the driver, but the driver refused to unload the family's belongings unless he was paid the sum he demanded. Soldiers witnessed the exchange and demanded that the driver accept the five dollars and give the family their things. When the driver refused the order, the soldiers held up a watch and gave the driver three minutes to comply. After the three minutes expired, the driver still refused to budge on the price, and the soldiers ran him through with their bayonets.

But deadly clashes were not just taking place between citizens and authorities; tension ran high between those keeping order as well. One such clash was reported by an eyewitness named Mr. Fast, who saw the encounter go down in Jefferson Square. There, a policeman and soldier argued over who should pick up a dead body and put it in the wagon. Both men ordered the other to do so, and when each refused, the exchange became heated. Finally, the soldier pulled out his gun and shot the policeman dead, right in the street.

The tension felt by the patrolmen tasked with defending the city from crime also led to some even more unfortunate stories of those being shot due to woeful misunderstandings. In one instance, a man who owned a grocery store saw that the fire was rapidly approaching and that his business would not be spared. So, he opened the doors and allowed anyone in the area to take what they wanted. This information was not known to a passing soldier, who, after seeing a man walk out of the store with groceries in his arms, assumed he was stealing. Without a word, he ran up to the innocent man and stabbed him with his bayonet.

A bank clerk, who was ordered to search the ruins of his bank, was mistaken for a looter and shot. There were also numerous regrettable stories of people being mistaken for looters and shot while going into their own homes.

Others were shot for the most minor of infractions, such as washing their hands in drinking water that was intended to ease the thirst of those gathered in a park. Two men tried to get around the mayor's order of keeping the city in darkness during the night and lit candles; soldiers shot them down through the windows of their respective homes. A woman who lit a fire on her cook stove was no also exception, for she too was shot.

Though children caught stealing were spared immediate death, they were not immune from the law or punishment for breaking it. Justice in those instances was meted out with a beating, after which the child was forced to wear a humiliating sign in public announcing "I am a thief."

Soldiers were not the only ones who executed the mayor's orders regarding looters. Some criminals fell by vigilante justice, doled out by citizens who would not stand idly by. One major example of this was performed by a group of miners near the Palace Hotel. When they found a man trying to rob a corpse, they took immediate action. Without waiting for any sort of authority figure, they took hold of the thief, found a rope, and promptly strung him up from a standing beam in the hotel ruins. Just moments later, the crowd caught a fellow criminal and quickly strung him up next to the first thief. The pair dangled together in the doorway, making for a grisly scene.

Baseless shootings also occurred when ordinary citizens took matters into their own hands. The final straw came when a citizens' patrol mistakenly shot Major H. C. Tilden and two others in his vehicle. The major, a prominent member of the General Relief Committee, was in a car that was being used as an ambulance, but the shooters claimed that they failed to see the Red Cross banner hung on the side. They also justified the shooting by saying that the vehicle hadn't stopped when they challenged it, but they also gave no lawful reason for having made the attempt in the first place. Tragically, Major Tilden died in the shooting, but his death became a catalyst for measures to be taken to curb the killings. Thereafter, an order was passed forbidding citizen patrols from carrying guns and even tightened regulations for soldiers using their weapons.

Virtually no incident during those few days was ever investigated in the aftermath. When all was said and done, sentries turned a blind eye to the deeds performed by their fellow patrolman and vigilante citizens, whether it was lawful or not.

Though the numerous stories make it seem like the city was practically lawless following the quake, for the most part, it was not. Truthfully, the strict order that was needed to get through the crisis was kept to, thanks mainly to a large and varied volunteer force of professionals that tirelessly patrolled the city. All in all, mass panic and major instances of crime were held at bay, and the city was prevented from descending into complete anarchy.

Chapter 8 – "Strangers in Our Own Streets"

"We were strangers in our own streets, refugees from our own houses."

—Henry A Lafler, Journalist

After fires had blazed across the city, the words Lafler expressed were felt by multitudes. Some half-crazed with fear, some stumbling about numbly, the suffering in the city was palpable. People struggled to find safety, medical assistance, or basic necessities. Some cried and called out for loved ones that were nowhere to be found.

Some "refugees" found help from kind strangers. Many of the affluent houses in the upper district had been initially spared destruction, so owners opened their homes and gathered up passing strangers who needed shelter and food. In one home, twenty refugees were allowed to sleep in the drawing room. The next morning, the owner took all that remained of her food stores—some flour and baking powder—and made breakfast for her hungry guests. But even this refuge would not provide a long-term place for safety. The fire was making its way into the neighborhood, and homeowners and refugees alike were forced to flee.

Despite the dynamite blasts used to slow or stop the fires, the movement of the conflagrations could not be wholly predicted. With many now homeless or fleeing fires that approached their neighborhoods, there were few places to find assured safety.

Thousands of people arrived at the ferry docks, many on foot, carrying what belongings they could and begging to be let onto the departing boats. Many had been forced to flee their homes without warning, so they had nothing with them and could not even afford the ten-cent fare to be taken across the bay. Those who had been able to pay the obscenely inflated prices (as much as $50) to be transported to the ferry by a driver were not guaranteed a chance to leave either.

From the ferry area, flames could be seen in the city all around, increasing the people's panic and urgency. G. A. Raymond, whose harrowing tale of escape was noted earlier, was one of the many who reached the ferry docks. He, like many others, believed that reaching the ferry would mean that they were saved. But upon arriving there, any hope for safety or comfort was soon shattered. Raymond described the scene as "bedlam, pandemonium, and hell rolled into one."

In his estimates, as many as ten thousand panicked people fought like wild animals to get on board the ferries Frantic survivors begged for safe passage and food while women fainted from thirst. People tore at each other, ripping the clothing from the backs of anyone in their way, and fear caused grown men to lose their reason. One man, who was rendered senseless from the chaos and anguish, beat his head on an iron pillar and shouted in agony, "The city must be saved!"

When the gates to the ferries were finally opened, further chaos ensued. The mad rush swept everyone within the crowd aboard the ferries, jamming people into every square inch of the boats. But as G. A. Raymond remarked, no one cared about the overcrowded conditions—there was only relief to be escaping the city.

Yet, as packed as the ferries were, not all were able to find space. Many more people remained on the dock, unable to board. As the last boat pulled away from the dock, frantic men and women made desperate attempts to jump aboard only to fall into the water, some possibly having jumped to their deaths.

Those who could not leave the city were compelled to find locales within it where the fire could not reach them. Without any source of shelter in the first few days and nights, both rich and poor, citizens and immigrants, were forced to camp out in the open within whatever safe zone they could reach. With the fires burning on the eastern part of the city, many migrated to the western side.

Some sought safety within the boundaries of the Presidio. Occupying 1,480 acres of land, the Presidio military installation was mostly open ground, containing few buildings or homes over its vast expanse. Though there was a chance fire would reach the forest within its areas, it was still a safer option than most.

Aside from the Presidio (which reached all the way to the Golden Gate Channel), many escaped to the open grounds of the nearby one-thousand-acre Golden Gate Park. From its sparsely populated surroundings down to the soft golden sand dunes that met the Pacific Ocean, the park became a safe haven to rest. It sat in a relatively peaceful juxtaposition to the fiery, charred ruins that many had fled.

Others sought a more macabre safety among the dead, camping out in graveyards and, where possible, sheltering in mausoleum-type vaults alongside the coffins of the deceased.

Smaller outdoor plazas and parks also served as a temporary refuge for those who reached them, though they may have felt somewhat less secure than in larger spaces like the Presidio or Golden Gate Park. Alta Plaza, sitting on the crest of a hill and taking up a relatively paltry area of four city blocks (twelve acres), was one such place. During the nights, refugees huddled together among their bundles of belongings, hellish fires burning brightly around them, turning the darkness to daylight. One man who spent a night in Alta

Plaza recalled seeing firefighters retreat into the plaza throughout the night, dropping down breathless with exhaustion. There was little in the way of food or water to revive them save for some emergency food and a few buckets of water reserved specifically for the returning heroes. However, a sergeant carried something that practically amounted to gold at the time—one precious bottle of whisky, which he gave to the tired firemen.

While men defended the city from fires and crime, the women stepped up to do their part. They comforted and cared for the needs of others, especially those who had been separated from spouses or children in the initial chaos. They displayed their own courage, self-sacrifice, and compassion when others needed it most.

Jane Tingley, a well-known writer, was one such heroine. She recounted one particularly heartbreaking story of coming across a disheveled, half-naked woman in Golden Gate Park. The woman, her stare fixed on the water beyond, repeated in a trance-like chant, "Here I am, my pretties. Come here, come here." Compassionately taking her by the hand, Jane brought the woman down the hill to her husband, who was weeping. Explaining his wife's state, he told Jane, "She is calling our three little children. She thinks the sounds of the ocean waves are the voices of our lost darlings." Having become separated from their young children during the rush to flee the fire, the parents had been searching all over for them, taking no time for food or rest. Of everyone they saw, they forlornly asked the same question, "Have you seen anything of our lost babies?" Yet, Jane knew that it might be days before the pitiful parents would have an answer as to what became of their children.

Lost children were not the only urgent issue that arose amidst the crisis. Unfortunately, for a number of heavily pregnant women, their unborn children decided to come into the world with some of the worst possible timing. Among the parks, the dunes, and the Presidio, babies were born out in the open with sparse medical assistance or equipment. One wealthy city resident, with the help of an amateur midwife, even gave birth on the front lawn of her mansion while the family waited for the dynamite squad to come and blow up their stately home. The midwife, on seeing the newborn open its eyes, wryly remarked, "God sends earthquakes and babies, but He might, in His mercy, cut out sending them both together."

According to Jane Tingley, nine new lives were ushered into the world that day. Eight babies were recorded being born in Buena Vista Park, but scholars believe many others were born in various locations around the city. Sadly, the mortality rate of the new mothers and babies was high, with many dying in the places they sought refuge.

However, not all of the new births had a tragic ending. Tingley recalled the night when a soldier begged her to go help another woman. Without telling her what was happening, he simply pointed her to a hedge of bushes. When she walked into the brush, she saw a crudely constructed shelter made with a blanket. Inside the shelter lay a woman naked in the grass, clothes torn and scattered around her. It was immediately evident to Jane that the poor woman, all alone, was in labor. Sending someone to find a doctor, she was soon joined by two other women who came to help. Although no doctor could be found, a medical student was sent over to assist. Of the baby's arrival, Tingley wrote, "Under the best ministrations we could find, a new life was ushered into this hell, which, a few hours before, was the fairest among cities."

Though within the first two days after the quake, many within the city were able to find safety and some form of shelter from the fire, more pressing needs soon arose as the city began to hunger and thirst.

Chapter 9 – Sweet Relief and Labors of Mercy

Though it was apparent to city officials early on that measures needed to be taken to prevent a famine from compounding the problems the city faced, implementing these steps would be more difficult. For two days, not one supply of food (or anything for that matter) was able to come into the city.

At first, the soldiers did what they could to find even the most meager supplies to feed the hungry people gathered in the squares by commandeering bread from bakeries or using emergency reserves. Military stores had adequate supplies and were opened to citizens. But with no way of receiving news or communication that these stores were open to the public, most were ignorant of the existence of these provisions and could not take advantage of them. But soon thereafter, General Frederick Funston used the food stocks in the Presidio and sent rations out to the city to be distributed among the hungry.

As the fires raged, quick-thinking officers and soldiers had all foodstuffs and supplies from grocery stores that were in danger of burning conveyed to safer locations. In total, 390 stores had their contents saved, with that food going to feed refugees in the coming days. Stores that remained open quickly ran low on supplies. It wasn't long before fresh foods disappeared, with those in the city relying on crackers and canned foods to assuage their hunger. Those who were able to buy food had to do so at a premium, as many store owners doubled their prices despite the order against price gouging.

As soldiers began collecting carcasses of dead animals around the city, grotesque rumors arose that the military was using these to feed refugees. It was patently false, but given what was happening on the shores of Lake Merced, the story almost seemed plausible. Hungry refugees around the lake, becoming desperate for food, spotted live ducks and swans the city kept as decorations. But looking less like adornments and more like a meal, several men jumped into the lake and swam after the waterfowl. Within a short time, every duck had been cooked and eaten.

But it was obvious that 300,000 people could not be sustained on city ducks and rescued crackers. Without action, famine would rage quickly on the heels of the doused fires.

Even more urgent was the matter of finding fresh drinking water for the city, without which death was only a matter of a few days away. Full reservoirs teased the people with its water, yet their distance and difficulty in being reached prevented them from being a quick solution. Still, something had to be done, so wagons were mounted with barrels of water and driven through the park, with soldiers guarding the precious commodity against the thirsty citizens eager to ease their suffering. But with a one drink per person allowance, the quenching of thirst was short-lived.

With the danger of famine looming in the days after the quake, Mayor Schmitz gave orders for "supplies to be given to those in need." That would be no small feat. On the afternoon of the great quake, Mayor Schmitz had already known that the city government was ill-equipped to handle a crisis of that magnitude. That day, he quickly gathered the city's most able lawyers, leaders, and businessmen and created the now well-known Committee of Fifty, which included the mayor himself as chairman.[4]

In the days following the quake, the committee was tasked with distributing food to the city. Word of the disaster had spread across the state and country, including even the federal government.[5] Within days, food, medical supplies, and other necessities began pouring into the city from all over California and the rest of the country. Trains and steamer ships arrived laden with necessities sent by civil organizations as well as other military bases. But all these supplies needed to be received, transported, and stored before distribution.

In less than a week, the relief effort had become too overwhelming for the Committee of Fifty, and the mayor turned to the army for help. The quartermaster of the Presidio, Major Carroll Devol, was charged with receiving, transporting, and distributing supplies from the outpost. General Adolphus Greely was asked to handle the enormous job of fairly distributing food to the thousands of citizens who desperately depended on them.

At first, Greely was reluctant to accept the assignment and refused. The Committee of Fifty pressed him to reconsider, and eventually, he relented. Greely got to work setting up nine food depots around the city while the Presidio cared for the sixteen thousand refugees who sought help within its confines.[6] Even though there were supplies coming into the city, food and water were strictly rationed, with each person receiving three-quarters of a soldier's ration.

---

[4] The Committee of Fifty has also been referred to as the Citizen's Committee of Fifty and the Citizen's Relief Committee.

[5] Money was also sent from various relief organizations, with the US government taking the lead in appropriating $1,000,000 to relief funds.

[6] This number is based on army reports. The army also reported that 30,000 citizens were so destitute that they were completely dependent on the army for food and shelter. However, in total, 300,000 were fed at army food stations on April 30th alone.

At first, the need for food was so great that it went out to be distributed as fast as it came in, with little thought given to balanced allocation. As long as it was food, it was going out to the people. Despite little initial organization, by the end of the week, the danger of famine had passed.

While the regular army worked to stave off the famine, the Army Corp of Engineers took on the duties of supplying water to the city. With the city's main waterlines shattered, not only clean drinking water but also sanitation moved up the list of growing priorities. Dr. Marcus Herstein, a member of the Committee of Fifty, pointed out that if the water mains were broken, there was no doubt that the sewer system had been decimated as well. He predicted that they would soon find the city "covered with the stumps of open sewer pipes." The rats would have easy access to all parts of the city, with "the main sewers as boulevards." Open sewers and rats were a potential health and hygiene nightmare, and it was a new potential disaster the city could ill afford.

Among the list of priorities was also shelter, something desperately needed by refugees who had fled their homes with nothing more than the thin covering of clothes on their backs. Air temperatures were mild, and camping in the park may not have seemed to be the worst option, but as luck would have it, severe rains moved in on the days following the quake, compounding the suffering of those who had lost their homes. Two nights that week, pouring rains soaked the poor unfortunate souls living out in the open. Even those who had crude shelters set up found them to be wholly inadequate against the deluge-like rains. All those outside during the storms ended up shivering and soaked to the bone, increasing the urgency for shelters.

Making sure that everyone received the needed food, water, and shelter was logistically difficult with such a fluid situation. Many homeless, having no permanent location, moved around the city, making it difficult to figure out how and where to effectively organize and meet everyone's needs. Thus, boundary lines were set, and six districts were created, breaking the areas up into territories that troops could be assigned to care for. As this organizational effort began, it became apparent that reinforcements were needed. A plea to the War Department led to an additional 1,500 troops and 45 officers being dispatched to the city to help with the relief.

The initial hasty relief effort soon started to give way to more organized provisions. One hundred thirty-five carpenters set to work building shelters. Eight large temporary shed-like structures were put up in Golden Gate Park, where a large bulk of the refugees camped. Thousands without tents were able to be housed in these, and though they were pretty rudimentary, they were much more comfortable than living in the open. As more structures were built, the designs also improved in small ways. Builders divided them into compartments, each with its own outside entrance. They were able to reasonably house a family and give them a bit of blessed privacy.

The military also issued a total of twenty-five thousand tents—some common tents but the majority being shelter tents—and these were also set up in Golden Gate Park, as well as other parks and open areas. More scattered tents in outlying areas were also systematically gathered into the camp system. Each camp had a number, and even the tents within were given numbers, a sort of temporary address that made conditions just a little homier.

Day by day, the camps continued to grow into completed systems. Lumber from a loaded schooner in the bay was commandeered and brought to the Engineer Corps to create tent floors, letting refugees get off the dirt and live in more comfortable conditions.

Once the shelters were up, the work did not end there. The camps, as organized as they became, were not like city neighborhoods with privately owned homes. They could not be left to administer themselves. Each camp had a military officer in charge of it with an army surgeon on-site responsible for medical needs as well as sanitation. Every camp was also assigned a Red Cross worker to deal with registering "residents," a process put in place to help organize the logistics of food, clothes, and other necessities each person or family would need.

While the camp system was being established, it was obvious to authorities that the food receiving and delivery system needed work. Major C. R. Krauthoff of the Subsistence Department had the unenviable task of smoothing out and perfecting that system. He would shortly devise a delivery system for food depots and relief camps. This system was set up in a way that ensured food supplies were more evenly distributed so that one camp didn't end up with all of the flour supplies and another with nothing but ham.

An abundance of water was also now being supplied to the camps. But with no water filtration or treatment system, they had to create a new one. So, the general hospital in each camp developed bacteria cultures that purified the water and rendered it fit for human consumption. Now, refugees not only had enough water to drink, but they could also bathe and wash. The camp even had a laundry service, which was sorely needed after days in the soot and dirt.

An interesting aspect of camp life had to do with social and cultural differences. Many who found themselves under a canvas in the dirt had just days before enjoyed the luxury of being served by butlers in their immaculate mansions. Now, the forces of nature had leveled the playing field for many. Both rich and poor, citizens and immigrants, suffered the same deprivations and lived under the same exact conditions for the first time in their lives. Tensions, differences in lifestyles, and differing backgrounds made it inevitable that incidents of rowdiness would break out as people trampled on the rights of others and showed disregard for commonly held decencies.

The closeness of camp life also gave rise to another inevitable problem—the easy spread of disease. However, the military's sanitation efforts were somewhat rewarded in this aspect. Though there were reported cases of typhoid fever and smallpox, there were no outbreaks on an epidemic level.

By the end of April, relief efforts were well in hand, with 300,000 people being cared for by authorities. The work wouldn't be over, though. There would be a massive effort to clean up and rebuild. And that cleanup effort would include the grim task of finding and burying the dead.

The bodies that had not been burned in the fire needed to be cared for quickly. Though the search and recovery started while the flames still raged, it would continue into the days after.

Taking care of the dead was perhaps the most heartbreaking and difficult of tasks. It was truly a labor of mercy, and not all did so willingly. Soldiers, police, and firemen were needed for other work, so citizens were drafted to help. Those who objected quickly found out that they did not have a choice in the matter, some staring down the barrel of a soldier's gun. Troops needed every capable male to pitch in, and they would not stand for dissension.

At first, bodies were conveyed to city squares, which served as temporary public morgues, a gruesome sight for those who sought safety from the fires. Those seeking sanctuary in places like Mechanics' Pavilion and Portsmouth Square would be further traumatized by the nearness of as many as twenty or thirty corpses laid together in the grass.

When fires began to threaten those areas, the necessity for quick burials arose so that the bodies were not lost to the flames. Other corpses were transported to the Presidio. But that required additional vehicles and drivers than soldiers had available. So, passing vehicles were pressed into service as sort of temporary hearses.

When the bodies began to pile up in the Presidio and other areas, they became a health hazard and required quick burials. A temporary cemetery was opened, and the grueling work of digging graves by hand was left both to those who did so voluntarily and those who were forcibly compelled. Rich and working class alike picked up spades and labored through the dirt, side by side. Once the graves were dug, the men lowered the bodies into the earth. There was no time for individual burials, so several bodies were placed into each grave.

Sadly, many of the dead were never identified and went to their final resting place unknown. Names of those who could be identified were written down, and those whose names were unknown had descriptions written of them in hopes their loved ones might be able to recognize them. Many went without the comfort of seeing their loved ones have a proper funeral.

Those who were buried with their loved ones present created a pitiable scene. Especially so was one young girl whose father, her only relative, died in the earthquake. As the body was brought from place to place, she followed until it finally came to rest in the Presidio. She watched as her father was buried at the outpost, weeping as other women tried to comfort her. Others wept for their loved ones alongside her, many kneeling on the ground as a Catholic priest performed funeral services throughout the day.

Chapter 10 – Rising from the Ashes

In the days and weeks that followed the great disaster, San Francisco underwent dramatic changes—even in less obvious ways. Many left the city during and after the crisis and didn't return, but those who stayed felt and displayed extraordinary comradery. Personal conflicts were put aside, racial barriers were broken down and forgotten, and social distinctions no longer mattered—everyone was on a level playing field.

For weeks after the disaster, the mayor upheld the order that no fires could be lit inside houses. Those with houses still standing brought stoves outside and cooked on sidewalks and in the streets. Those who previously had servants to prepare meals now had to fend for themselves, and even the most well-heeled and highly educated women prepared meals under the sky.

For those that remained in the camps for the months and years following the earthquake, they began to establish regular routines, their lives taking on a somewhat normal tone with gatherings in dining halls and children playing with newfound friends. The city had union carpenters build cottages (5,300 in total), dubbed "earthquake shacks," for the newly homeless, which allowed the people to slowly move out of tents and into their new lives.

Marriages around the city skyrocketed as women were left homeless by the disaster, now turning to their fiancés to give them a home. New life continued to emerge, even in unlikely places—a baby was born behind some screens on the sidewalk in front of his parents' mansion, and in the same night, the next block over, a litter of kittens was born to a lost cat.

Dr. Herstein's fears regarding rats and the spread of disease were legitimate, as bubonic plague broke out in the city and not just among the homeless or immigrant communities. In total, there were 160 cases confirmed, and 14 died in one month.

Many praised the mayor, some raising him to near hero status after his handling of the crisis. Even regular critics like those at the *Bulletin* suspended its critical comments about the mayor in the weeks that followed. They were not the only ones to put aside political rivalries in the interest of rebuilding. As the *Bulletin* noted, "the fire burned out old enmities" between political factions, and the paper remained committed to cooperating "with the men who are laying the foundations of the new San Francisco."

Those men in charge of the rebuilding formed a new city committee. The Committee of Fifty was disbanded and replaced with the Committee of Forty on the Reconstruction of San Francisco, headed by Abraham "Boss" Ruef. One of the reconstruction efforts the city underwent involved the heavily damaged water supply system. From this, a better system arose, and construction of the city's Auxiliary Water Supply System—the largest high-pressure water distribution system ever built—was underway.

Regarding the changes the city underwent and would continue to undergo, author and journalist William Henry Owen mused, "Old San Francisco is dead...It is as though a pretty, frivolous woman has passed through a great tragedy. She survives, but she is sobered and different. If it rises out of the ashes, it must be a modern city." And arise from the ashes it did.

Conclusion

The great earthquake of 1906 was so intense that it was picked up by seismographs around the world, such as in Tokyo, Moscow, Berlin, Cape Town, and London. According to US Army reports at the time, there were 498 deaths in San Francisco; however, later reports by the National Oceanic and Atmospheric Agency (NOAA) estimate it could have been more like 700 to 800 (though, by some calculations, even those numbers underestimate the casualties San Francisco endured).

Though her damage was severe, San Francisco was not the only city that suffered. It is estimated that there were more than three thousand deaths caused directly or indirectly by the earthquake, including the more than one hundred people who died when the walls of Agnews State Asylum crumbled atop them.

Twenty-eight thousand buildings and around five hundred city blocks (4.7 square miles) were destroyed, leaving 225,000 people homeless and causing over $400 million in damages, making it one of the costliest and deadliest earthquakes in US history.[7]

---

[7] Today that would equate to around $8.2 billion.

Here's another book by Captivating History
that you might like

Free Bonus from Captivating History (Available for a Limited time)

Hi History Lovers!

Now you have a chance to join our exclusive history list so you can get your first history ebook for free as well as discounts and a potential to get more history books for free! Simply visit the link below to join.

Captivatinghistory.com/ebook

Also, make sure to follow us on Facebook, Twitter and Youtube by searching for Captivating History.

References

Anderson, Michael. *Frederick Funston: The Man Who Saved San Francisco.*

www.parks.ca.gov/.

Bean, Walton (1974). *Boss Ruef's San Francisco: The Story of the Union Labor Party, Big Business, and the Graft Prosecution.* Berkeley: University of California Press. https://archive.org/details/bossruefssanfran00bean/page/122/mode/2up.

Bronson, William (2014). *The Earth Shook, The Sky Burned: A Photographic Record of the 1906 San Francisco Earthquake and Fire.* Edition:100th. Publisher: Chronicle Books LLC.

Death of Fire Chief Engineer Dennis T. Sullivan. Virtual Museum of the City of San Francisco. Archived from the original on 2013-06-17. Retrieved 2021-3-10. http://www.sfmuseum.net/hist10/dtsullivan.html.

Dr. William Ellsworth Wallace, R.R. (ed.). *The San Andreas Fault System.* California, USGS Professional Paper 1515, Denver, CO, 283 pp., paperback, 1990.

Ellsworth, W.L., 1990, Earthquake history, 1769-1989, chap. 6 of Wallace, R.E., ed., The San Andreas Fault System, California: U.S. Geological Survey Professional Paper 1515, p. 152-187. The Great

1906 San Francisco Earthquake
https://earthquake.usgs.gov/earthquakes/events/1906calif/18april/.

Fradkin, Philip L., *The Great Earthquake and Firestorms of 1906*, Archived June 9, 2007, at the Wayback Machine.

History of the Presidio. www.presidio.gov/visit/history-of-the-presidio.

Lomax, A., (2005), A Reanalysis of the Hypocentral Location and Related Observations for the Great 1906 California Earthquake, *Bull. Seism. Soc. Am.*, 95, 861-877.

National Park Service, *From Presidio of San Francisco*

National Park Service; Agnews Insane Asylum
www.nps.gov/places/agnews-insane-asylum.htm.

Schulz, Sandra S.; Wallace, Robert E. *The San Andreas Fault.* https:pubs.usgs.gov/.

Strobridge, William, *Soldiers in the Streets.* The Pacific Historian 22.1 (Spring 1978): 4

Thatcher, Wayne (December 10, 1975). *Strain accumulation and release mechanism of the 1906 San Francisco Earthquake. Journal of Geophysical Research.* 80 (35): 4862–4872. Bibcode:1975JGR....80.4862T..

Thomas S. Duke (1910) *Synopsis of the San Francisco Police and Municipal records of the Greatest Catastrophe in American History.* Published with Approval of the Honorable Board of Police Commissioners of San Francisco 1910

Thomas, Gordon; Morgan Witts, Max (1933, 1971) *The San Francisco Earthquake.* New York, Stein and Day
https://archive.org/details/sanfranciscoeart00thom/page/56/mode/2up.

USGS, *Casualties and damage after the 1906 Earthquake, United States Geological Survey.*
https://earthquake.usgs.gov/earthquakes/events/1906calif/18april/casualties.php.

Wallace, Gregory (2014) *The 10 Most Expensive U.S. Earthquakes.* https://money.cnn.com/2014/08/24/news/economy/earthquakes-10-most-expensive/index.html.

Made in the USA
Coppell, TX
11 June 2021